Netwo Administrator's Guide

Practical Guide

A. De Quattro

Network Administrator's Guide

Chapter 1: Introduction

1.1 What is a Network Administrator?

A network administrator is a professional responsible for the management, maintenance, and operational efficiency of computer networks within an organization. These networks can include local area networks (LANs), wide area networks (WANs), and cloud networks that facilitate the communication between various systems, devices, and users. The role of a network administrator is crucial in ensuring that a company's IT infrastructure is robust, secure, and capable of supporting the organization's strategic goals.

Network administrators typically work in various sectors, such as corporate offices, educational institutions, hospitals, and government agencies, and their function remains vital in almost all environments where the exchange of information is necessary. The responsibilities of a network administrator encompass a broad range of tasks, from installing and configuring network equipment to troubleshooting connectivity issues and ensuring compliance with security protocols.

In an era characterized by rapid technological advancement and increased reliance on interconnected devices, the demand for skilled network administrators has surged. Their expertise enables organizations to leverage networking technologies effectively and promote efficient workflows. As organizations become more data-driven, the need for network administrators who can manage bandwidth, maintain network performance, safeguard against cyber threats, and foster seamless communication is paramount.

1.2 Role and Responsibilities

The role of a network administrator is multifaceted. While specific duties may vary depending on the organization's size and industry, the fundamental responsibilities typically include the following:

1. **Network Design and Deployment**: Network administrators are involved in designing the layout of a network, selecting appropriate hardware and software, and deploying systems that meet the organization's needs. This may involve creating architectures that can handle a high volume of traffic, consider redundancy, or offer specific functionalities.

2. **Configuration and Installation**: They are responsible for installing and configuring network devices such as routers, switches, firewalls, and access points. Proper configuration ensures devices operate correctly within the network, connecting users efficiently.

3. **Monitoring Network Performance**: Network administrators continuously monitor the performance of the network to ensure optimal functionality. They utilize various tools and software solutions to track metrics such as data traffic, device connectivity, and bandwidth utilization.

4. **Network Security Management**: Protecting the network from unauthorized access, malware, and cyber attacks is a critical responsibility. Network administrators implement security measures, enforce policies, and regularly update systems to safeguard sensitive information and maintain compliance with regulations.

5. **Troubleshooting Issues**: When network problems arise, network administrators should be able to identify the root cause and resolve issues swiftly. This could involve diagnosing hardware

malfunctions, software glitches, or connectivity problems, often requiring a systematic approach to problem-solving.

6. **User Support and Training**: Network administrators provide support to end-users experiencing networking issues. They may also conduct training sessions to educate users on best practices and how to leverage network resources effectively.

7. **Documentation and Reporting**: Maintaining documentation of network configurations, procedures, and incidents is vital for future reference and troubleshooting. Network administrators also produce reports detailing network performance and incidents to inform management and stakeholders.

8. **Upgrading Infrastructure**: As technology evolves, network infrastructure requires updates to remain efficient and secure. Network administrators plan for and

implement upgrades to hardware and software as necessary to support organizational growth.

9. **Collaboration with Other IT Staff**: Network administrators often work closely with system administrators, cybersecurity experts, and other IT professionals to ensure that all aspects of the IT environment are integrated and functioning well.

10. **Capacity Planning and Management**: Ensuring that the network can handle current and anticipated loads is crucial. Administrators evaluate usage patterns and make recommendations for enhancements to accommodate growth.

1.3 Required Skills

Becoming a proficient network administrator requires a combination of technical knowledge, problem-solving capabilities, and interpersonal skills. Key competencies include:

1. **Technical Proficiency**: A thorough understanding of networking concepts, protocols (such as TCP/IP, DHCP, and DNS), and hardware components is essential. Familiarity with networking devices and their configuration is also critical.

2. **Networking Certifications**: While formal education (such as a degree in computer science or information technology) can be beneficial, certifications such as Cisco's CCNA (Cisco Certified Network Associate), CompTIA Network+, and Microsoft Certified: Azure Fundamentals affirm expertise and understanding of network administration.

3. **Cybersecurity Awareness**: Given the rising threat of cyberattacks, network administrators should have a solid grasp of

security principles, including firewalls, intrusion detection systems, and VPNs (Virtual Private Networks).

4. **Analytical Skills**: The ability to analyze data and identify trends is vital for monitoring network performance and troubleshooting issues. A methodical approach is necessary for diagnosing problems.

5. **Problem-Solving Abilities**: Network administrators must think critically to resolve unforeseen technical challenges. Their capacity to find effective solutions swiftly is an essential aspect of the role.

6. **Communication Skills**: Since network administrators often liaise with users, management, and other IT professionals, excellent verbal and written communication skills are essential. They must be able to explain complex technical concepts in

layman's terms to facilitate understanding.

7. **Attention to Detail**: Maintaining network configurations, security policies, and documentation requires a keen eye for detail to prevent errors that could lead to significant disruptions.

8. **Time Management**: Network administrators manage multiple tasks simultaneously, ranging from routine maintenance to urgent troubleshooting. Efficient time management skills are necessary to balance these responsibilities effectively.

9. **Adaptability**: The IT landscape is continuously evolving, with the introduction of new technologies and practices. Network administrators must be willing to learn and adapt to stay relevant in their field.

10. **Customer Service Orientation**: Providing exceptional support to users contributes to overall satisfaction with the network resources. A focus on customer service enhances user confidence in the network's reliability.

Chapter 2: Network Architecture

In this chapter, we delve into the intricacies of network architecture, discussing various types of networks, network models, and the topologies that define how these networks are structured. Understanding these components is vital for anyone involved in networking, whether in a theoretical capacity or practical implementation.

2.1 Types of Networks

The classification of networks can be done based on various criteria such as size, coverage area, and purpose. Here, we explore three primary types: Local Area Networks (LAN), Wide Area Networks (WAN), and Metropolitan Area Networks (MAN).

2.1.1 Local Area Networks (LAN)

Local Area Networks (LANs) are networks that connect computers and devices within a limited geographical area, such as a home, school, or office building. This type of network is characterized by its high data transfer rates, typically ranging from 10 Mbps to 10 Gbps, and low latency.

Key Characteristics of LANs:

- **Geographical Coverage**: LANs usually span a small area—usually under a few kilometers.

- **Ownership**: They are typically owned, controlled, and managed by a single organization or individual.

- **High-speed connectivity**: LANs often employ Ethernet or Wi-Fi technologies to facilitate high-speed data transfer.

- **Cost-effective**: Setting up LANs is generally less expensive compared to wide area networks, making them an attractive choice for smaller entities.

Common Uses of LANs:

- **Home Networking**: Connecting personal computers, smartphones, tablets, smart home devices, and gaming consoles.

- **Business Networks**: Facilitating connectivity among computers in an office environment, enabling resource sharing such as printers and file storage.

2.1.2 Wide Area Networks (WAN)

Wide Area Networks (WANs) extend over a broad geographical area, connecting multiple LANs and other types of networks. These networks are often used to connect branches of an organization that are situated far away from each other.

Key Characteristics of WANs:

- **Geographical Coverage**: WANs can cover cities, countries, or even continents.

- **Ownership and Management**: WANs may be owned by multiple organizations; they often rely on intermediate connections leased from telecommunications providers.

- **Lower Data Speed**: Data transfer rates on WANs are generally slower than LANs due to their wide reach and the technologies used, with typical speeds ranging from 56 Kbps to 1 Gbps.

- **Complex Infrastructure**: WANs utilize a variety of technologies such as MPLS, frame relay, and leased lines, often depending on the distance and data needs.

Common Uses of WANs:

- **Corporate Networking**: Linking different branches of a business to enable seamless communication and resource sharing.

- **Internet Access**: The global Internet

itself is essentially the largest and most complex WAN, allowing for data exchange across the world.

2.1.3 Metropolitan Area Networks (MAN)

Metropolitan Area Networks (MANs) occupy an intermediary position between LANs and WANs, typically covering a city or a large campus. They play an essential role in connecting various LANs within a specific geographical region.

Key Characteristics of MANs:

- **Geographical Coverage**: MANs generally cover a range of 5 to 50 kilometers, making them suitable for urban environments.

- **Ownership**: Generally constructed and owned by a consortium of businesses or government institutions, with some services also provided by telephone or cable companies.

- **Intermediate Speed**: Data transfer rates in MANs often range from 1 Mbps to 10 Gbps.

Common Uses of MANs:

- **City-wide Networks**: Providing connectivity for businesses within a city, enabling data sharing and communication.

- **Public Internet Access**: Some cities implement MANs to provide Wi-Fi services across public spaces, enhancing accessibility.

2.2 Network Models

Understanding the different network models is crucial for effective networking design and implementation. The two primary models discussed in this section are the OSI model and the TCP/IP model.

2.2.1 OSI Model

Developed by the International Organization for Standardization (ISO), the Open Systems Interconnection (OSI) model is a conceptual framework used to understand network interactions in seven distinct layers.

The Seven Layers of the OSI Model:

1. **Physical Layer**: This layer handles the physical connection between devices and is concerned with the transmission and reception of unstructured raw data over a physical medium.

2. **Data Link Layer**: The second layer is responsible for error detection and correction from the physical layer and handles the framing of the packets.

3. **Network Layer**: This layer is tasked

with routing data from sender to receiver through various networks and determines how the data is sent to the destination.

4. **Transport Layer**: Responsible for end-to-end communication, this layer ensures complete data transfer with methods for error correction and data delivery confirmation.

5. **Session Layer**: This layer establishes, maintains, and terminates communication sessions, handling the exchange of information between applications.

6. **Presentation Layer**: Responsible for data translation and formatting, encryption, and compression, ensuring that data sent from the application layer of one system is readable by the application layer of another.

7. **Application Layer**: The top layer provides network services directly to user

applications, encompassing protocols like HTTP, FTP, and SMTP.

Importance of the OSI Model:

The OSI model provides a universal language for networking, allowing different types of hardware and software to communicate with each other effectively.

2.2.2 TCP/IP Model

The TCP/IP model, also known as the Internet Protocol Suite, is a more simplified and practical model that comprises four layers and is specifically designed for networking over the Internet.

The Four Layers of the TCP/IP Model:

1. **Link Layer**: This layer is equivalent to the OSI's physical and data link layers, dealing with the link between the device and

the network via physical technologies like Ethernet or Wi-Fi.

2. **Internetwork Layer**: It corresponds to the OSI's network layer, focusing on routing packets of data across different networks.

3. **Transport Layer**: This layer is responsible for ensuring accurate data transfer, similar to OSI's transport layer, using protocols such as TCP and UDP.

4. **Application Layer**: The top layer incorporates the functions of OSI's session, presentation, and application layers, providing application services to the user, utilizing various protocols for web browsing, email, and file transfer.

Importance of the TCP/IP Model:

The TCP/IP model is foundational to the

Internet, facilitating the communication between computers regardless of their underlying hardware.

2.3 Network Topologies

Network topology refers to the arrangement of different elements in a network. The design influences performance, reliability, and scalability. This section explores three common types of topologies: star, ring, and bus.

2.3.1 Star Topology

In a star topology, all devices are connected to a central hub or switch. This layout is one of the most popular topologies in modern networking.

Characteristics of Star Topology:

- **Centralized Management**: The central hub manages communication amongst devices, simplifying troubleshooting and management.

- **Scalability**: New devices can easily be added without disrupting the network.

- **High Reliability**: If one device fails, it does not affect the rest of the network.

Drawbacks:

- **Dependency on Central Device**: If the central hub fails, the entire network becomes inoperable.

2.3.2 Ring Topology

In a ring topology, each device is connected to two other devices, forming a circular path for data transmission. This means data travels in one direction, from one device to the next until it reaches its destination.

Characteristics of Ring Topology:

- **Equal Access**: Each device on the network has an equal opportunity to communicate.

- **Predictable Data Transmission**: Data packets travel in a unidirectional manner, which can help in managing the flow of data.

Drawbacks:

- **Network Failure**: If any one device fails, the entire network can suffer unless corrective measures (like dual ring) are implemented.

2.3.3 Bus Topology

In a bus topology, all devices share a single communication line or cable. Data is sent in both directions, with terminators at each end of the cable to prevent signal reflection.

Characteristics of Bus Topology:

- **Cost-effective**: Fewer cables and equipment are needed, making it cheaper to implement.

- **Easy to Set Up**: It's relatively straightforward to set up a bus network.

Drawbacks:

- **Limited Length**: There is a limit to the length of the bus, and as more devices are added, the performance can degrade.

- **Difficult to Troubleshoot**: Pinpointing issues can be challenging due to the shared communication line.

Conclusion

Understanding network architecture, including types of networks, models, and topologies, is essential for modern IT professionals. This chapter outlines fundamental concepts that influence network design and management. As technology continues to evolve, so too will the complexity and capabilities of network architecture, making it imperative for professionals to stay informed and adaptable. Through this knowledge, organizations can create robust, scalable, and efficient networks to support their needs.

This chapter serves as a foundation for deeper exploration into specific technologies and practices that are shaped by the principles outlined here. At its core, mastering network architecture is about facilitating communication and connectivity among devices, and ensuring that these interactions are as efficient and secure as possible. As such, effective networking is integral to both individual and organizational success in an increasingly interconnected world.

Chapter 3: Network Components

The infrastructure that underpins computer networking is complex yet fascinating, consisting of various devices, cables, connectors, and protocols that work in unison to create seamless communication between computers and other devices. In this chapter, we will explore the fundamental components of networks, delving into network devices like routers, switches, hubs, and access points, as well as the different types of cables and connectors used for data transmission. Additionally, we will address the importance of physical security in network environments.

3.1 Network Devices

Network devices are essential for communication and data exchange within a network. Each of these devices plays a unique role, contributing to the overall functionality and performance of the network.

3.1.1 Router

A router is a crucial device that connects multiple networks and directs data traffic between them. It serves as a gateway between a local network (such as a home or office network) and the internet. Routers use routing tables and protocols to determine the best path for data packets to reach their destination.

Modern routers come equipped with various features:

- **Network Address Translation (NAT):** NAT allows multiple devices within a local network to share a single public IP address, thereby conserving IP addresses and enhancing security by hiding internal IP addresses from external networks.

- **Firewall Capabilities:** Many routers include built-in firewall functionalities that protect the network from unauthorized access and potential threats.

- **Quality of Service (QoS):** QoS settings prioritize network traffic, ensuring that bandwidth is allocated to critical applications and services, thereby improving performance.

- **Wireless Capabilities:** Most contemporary routers offer wireless connectivity, enabling devices to connect to the network without physical cables.

- **Security Protocols:** Routers support various security protocols like WPA2 and WPA3, which encrypt data transmitted over wireless connections to protect against eavesdropping.

3.1.2 Switch

A switch is a network device that connects multiple devices within a single local area network (LAN). Unlike routers, which operate at the network layer, switches operate at the data link layer (Layer 2), where they use MAC addresses to forward data to the correct destination within the network.

Key features of switches include:

- **Data Packet Forwarding:** Switches receive incoming data packets and determine the destination MAC address to forward the packets only to the specific device that needs them, thus minimizing unnecessary data traffic and improving network efficiency.

- **VLAN Support:** Many switches support Virtual Local Area Networks (VLANs), allowing network administrators to segment networks logically for better traffic management and security.

- **Auto-negotiation:** Switches can automatically detect and adjust to the highest possible speed and duplex mode of connected devices.

- **Layer 3 Switching:** Some advanced switches also perform routing functions, allowing them to operate at Layer 3 (Network Layer) and providing both switching and routing capabilities.

3.1.3 Hub

A hub is one of the simplest networking devices, functioning as a central connection point for devices in a LAN. Unlike switches, hubs operate at Layer 1 (Physical Layer) and do not filter or direct data packets based on MAC addresses. Instead, they broadcast incoming data packets to all connected devices.

Hub characteristics include:

- **Simplicity:** Hubs are easy to install and configure, making them a low-cost option for connecting multiple devices in a small network.

- **Collision Domain:** All devices connected to a hub share the same collision domain, which can lead to network collisions and decreased performance as traffic increases.

- **Half-Duplex Communication:** Most hubs only support half-duplex communication, meaning data can either be sent or received at any given time, but not simultaneously.

Hubs have largely been replaced by switches in modern networks due to their limitations in traffic management and efficiency.

3.1.4 Access Point

An access point (AP) is a device that allows wireless devices to connect to a wired network. It acts as a bridge between the wired Ethernet network and wireless clients, such as laptops, smartphones, and tablets. Access points play a vital role in expanding the coverage area of a network.

Significant aspects of access points include:

- **Wireless Standards:** Access points support various wireless standards, such as Wi-Fi 5 (802.11ac) and Wi-Fi 6 (802.11ax), which dictate data rates, frequency bands, and protocols for connectivity.

- **Coverage Area:** The range of an access point can vary based on factors such as its transmission power, the environment, and the presence of physical obstructions.

- **Multiple SSIDs:** Many access points can broadcast multiple Service Set Identifiers (SSIDs), allowing network administrators to create separate networks for different user groups (e.g., guest networks).

- **Mesh Networking:** Some modern access points support mesh networking, which enables multiple APs to work together seamlessly, extending coverage and improving network reliability.

3.2 Cables and Connectors

The physical infrastructure of a network is

built on a foundation of cables and connectors, which facilitate the transmission of data between devices. Different types of cables and connectors serve varied purposes and are chosen based on criteria such as transmission distance, bandwidth requirements, and installation environment.

3.2.1 Ethernet Cables

Ethernet cables are the most common type of networking cable used to connect devices within a local area network. They come in various categories (Cat) that support different data transfer speeds and distances. The most widely used categories include:

- **Cat5e:** Capable of supporting speeds up to 1 Gbps (Gigabit Ethernet) over a distance of up to 100 meters, Cat5e cables are suitable for most home and small office networks.

- **Cat6:** Supporting speeds up to 10 Gbps over shorter distances (up to 55 meters), Cat6 cables include improved insulation to reduce crosstalk and interference.

- **Cat6a:** Capable of supporting 10 Gbps speeds over longer distances (up to 100 meters), Cat6a cables provide enhanced shielding for better performance in noisy environments.

- **Cat7 and Cat8:** These higher-grade cables are designed for specialized applications, offering even greater speeds and reduced interference, making them suitable for data centers and high-performance networking environments.

Connectors used with Ethernet cables typically include:

- **RJ45 Connectors:** The standard

connector for Ethernet cables, RJ45 connectors enable the physical connection between devices and network interfaces.

- **Other Connectors:** Depending on the application, other types of connectors may be used, such as fiber optic connectors for high-speed data transmission.

3.2.2 Fiber Optic Cables

Fiber optic cables utilize light to transmit data, allowing for faster speeds and greater bandwidth over longer distances without signal loss. Unlike copper cables, fiber optic cables are immune to electromagnetic interference, making them ideal for environments with heavy electronic equipment.

Types of fiber optic cables include:

- **Single-Mode Fiber (SMF):** Single-mode fiber is designed for long-distance communication, allowing data to travel over many kilometers without significant loss. It uses a small core diameter and a single light wavelength.

- **Multi-Mode Fiber (MMF):** Multi-mode fiber is suitable for shorter distances, typically within a building or campus. It has a larger core diameter, allowing multiple wavelengths of light to be transmitted simultaneously.

Connectors compatible with fiber optic cables include:

- **SC (Subscriber Connector):** SC connectors are widely used in network applications for their simple push-pull design.

- **LC (Lucent Connector):** LC connectors are smaller than SC connectors, allowing for higher port density in network equipment.

- **ST (Straight Tip):** ST connectors feature a bayonet-style coupling mechanism and are commonly used in legacy networks.

3.3 Physical Security of the Network

Physical security is a critical aspect of network integrity and reliability. It involves protecting the physical components of a network, such as servers, switches, and cables, from unauthorized access, damage, or theft. The following strategies and practices contribute to robust physical security in network environments:

3.3.1 Access Control

Implementing access control measures restricts physical access to network hardware. Strategies include:

- **Lock and Key Systems:** Ensure that areas where networking equipment is stored are locked and accessible only to authorized personnel.

- **Keycard Access:** Use electronic keycard systems to control entry to server rooms and network closets, providing an audit trail of who accessed these areas.

3.3.2 Surveillance

Surveillance systems play a vital role in monitoring access points within a network facility:

- **CCTV Cameras:** Installing closed-circuit television (CCTV) cameras in strategic locations helps deter unauthorized access and provides valuable evidence in case of a security breach.

- **Motion Sensors:** Coupling cameras with motion sensors can trigger alerts when unauthorized movement is detected in sensitive areas.

3.3.3 Environmental Controls

Maintaining ideal environmental conditions for network devices is crucial for their operation:

- **Temperature and Humidity Monitoring:** Use environmental monitoring systems to track temperature and humidity levels in server rooms, as extreme conditions can damage equipment.

- **Power Supply Management:** Implement uninterruptible power supplies (UPS) to protect against power surges and outages, ensuring that equipment remains operational.

3.3.4 Data Protection and Disposal

Proper data protection and disposal methods prevent unauthorized access to sensitive data:

- **Data Encryption:** Encrypt sensitive data both in transit and at rest to protect it from unauthorized access.

- **Secure Disposal:** Use secure data wiping methods for outdated hardware, ensuring that data cannot be recovered after disposal.

In summary, the network components outlined in this chapter play a critical role in enabling communication and ensuring seamless data transmission across various devices. From the fundamental devices such as routers, switches, and access points to the essential cables and connectors that facilitate connectivity, each element contributes to the overall functionality and security of the network. Slacking on physical security within network infrastructures can expose organizations to risks that threaten data integrity; therefore, implementing best practices in physical security is crucial for safeguarding network resources. As technology evolves, the importance of understanding and effectively managing these components continues to grow, reflecting the dynamic landscape of networking and cybersecurity.

Chapter 4: Network Protocols and Configuration

Network protocols play a crucial role in the functioning of any modern communication system, serving as the rules and conventions that govern how data is transmitted over networks. The configuration of these networks further assists in optimizing their operation and ensures seamless communication among interconnected devices. In this chapter, we explore the main network protocols, the principles behind IP addressing, the mechanics of DHCP, and the functionality provided by DNS.

4.1 Main Network Protocols

Understanding the key protocols that facilitate communication over networks is essential for anyone in the field of networking. The three main protocols we'll discuss in this section are Internet Protocol (IP), Transmission Control

Protocol (TCP), and User Datagram Protocol (UDP).

4.1.1 IP (Internet Protocol)

Internet Protocol, or IP, is a fundamental layer of the Internet protocol suite, responsible for addressing and routing packets of data so that they can travel across networks. Each device connected to the network is assigned a unique IP address, which serves as its identifier.

4.1.1.1 IP Addressing

IP addresses, which come in two versions – IPv4 and IPv6 – are essential for identifying devices on a network. IPv4 addresses are 32-bit numbers, expressed in decimal format as four groups of digits (e.g., 192.168.1.1). Due to the growing number of devices connected to the internet, IPv6 was introduced, utilizing 128 bits and allowing for an extraordinarily large number of unique IP addresses.

4.1.1.2 Routing

Routing is the process of selecting paths in a network along which data packets travel. IP defines the packet structure and the addressing that allows routers to transmit data effectively from the source to the destination. Routers interpret the destination IP addresses in the packets to determine the appropriate network path, making decisions based on their routing tables.

4.1.2 TCP (Transmission Control Protocol)

Transmission Control Protocol (TCP) is a key transport layer protocol designed to ensure reliable transmission of data across networks. It is connection-oriented, meaning a connection must be established between the communicating devices before data can be sent.

4.1.2.1 Reliability

TCP provides reliable communication through several mechanisms, including error detection, acknowledgment of received packets, and retransmission of lost packets. When data is sent, TCP divides it into segments, which are numbered sequentially. The receiving device sends back acknowledgments for successfully received segments, allowing the sender to keep track of what has been received and what still needs to be sent.

4.1.2.2 Flow Control and Congestion Control

TCP employs flow control and congestion control mechanisms to enhance the efficiency of data transmission. Flow control ensures that a sender does not overwhelm a receiving device by sending data faster than it can process. Congestion control helps prevent network congestion, which can lead to packet loss and delays, by monitoring the network's status and adjusting transmission rates accordingly.

4.1.3 UDP (User Datagram Protocol)

Unlike TCP, User Datagram Protocol (UDP) is a connectionless protocol, which means that there is no need for establishing a connection before data transfer. UDP is used primarily in scenarios where speed is critical, and some loss of data can be tolerated.

4.1.3.1 Advantages of UDP

One of the main advantages of UDP is its low latency. Applications such as video streaming, online gaming, and VoIP (Voice over Internet

Protocol) prefer UDP because they require timely delivery of data rather than guaranteed delivery. Although UDP does not provide reliability mechanisms like error checking and acknowledgment, its lightweight nature allows for faster data transmission.

4.1.3.2 Applications of UDP

UDP is well-suited for applications where the timely delivery of information is more crucial than the reliability of the data. For instance, live broadcasts, gaming, and real-time communication applications often leverage UDP for its efficiency.

4.2 IP Configuration

IP configuration refers to the assignment of IP addresses to devices on a network. There are two primary methods for this configuration: static addressing and dynamic addressing.

4.2.1 Static vs. Dynamic Addressing

4.2.1.1 Static IP Addressing

In static IP addressing, a device is assigned a fixed IP address that does not change. This method is commonly used for servers, printers, and other devices where a consistent IP address is necessary for proper communication. The main advantage of static addressing is its simplicity in management for devices that require uninterrupted accessibility.

However, static addressing can be cumbersome in larger networks, as it requires manual configuration for each device. This could lead to potential errors, such as IP conflicts, if two devices are mistakenly assigned the same address.

4.2.1.2 Dynamic IP Addressing

Dynamic IP addressing simplifies network management by using DHCP (Dynamic Host Configuration Protocol) to automatically assign IP addresses from a predefined pool to devices on the network. When a device connects to the network, it requests an IP address from the DHCP server, which dynamically allocates an available address.

Dynamic addressing not only reduces the need for manual assignments but also optimizes the use of IP addresses on the network. However, because the IP addresses are not permanent, devices may receive different IP addresses each time they connect.

4.3 DHCP (Dynamic Host Configuration Protocol)

Dynamic Host Configuration Protocol

(DHCP) automates the process of IP address assignment. It is a client-server protocol that provides a framework for devices to obtain network configuration information.

4.3.1 DHCP Process

The DHCP process involves several steps:

1. **DHCP Discover**: When a new device connects to the network, it broadcasts a DHCP Discover message to find DHCP servers.

2. **DHCP Offer**: DHCP servers that receive the Discover message respond with a DHCP Offer, which includes an available IP address and other configuration details.

3. **DHCP Request**: The device then sends a DHCP Request message indicating its acceptance of one of the offers it received.

4. **DHCP Acknowledgment**: The server responds with a DHCP Acknowledgment, confirming the IP address allocation and providing additional configuration information such as the subnet mask, default gateway, and DNS servers.

4.3.2 Lease Time

IP addresses assigned via DHCP are typically temporary, with a lease time that defines how long the address can be used before it must be renewed. This ensures efficient utilization of IP addresses and allows for greater flexibility as devices join and leave the network.

4.3.3 Advantages of DHCP

The advantages of using DHCP are numerous, including:

- **Centralized Management**: DHCP allows network administrators to manage IP address assignment from a central server, simplifying device management.

- **Reduced Configuration Errors**: Automatic allocation minimizes the chance of manual errors, such as IP conflicts.

- **Efficient IP Address Utilization**: By dynamically assigning addresses, organizations can make optimal use of their limited IP address space.

4.4 DNS (Domain Name System)

The Domain Name System (DNS) is a crucial component of the Internet that translates human-readable domain names (like www.example.com) into IP addresses (like

192.0.2.1) that computers can read. DNS essentially acts as the phonebook of the Internet, allowing users to access websites using easy-to-remember names rather than numeric addresses.

4.4.1 How DNS Works

When a user enters a domain name in their web browser, the following steps typically occur:

1. **Query**: The browser first checks its local cache to see if it has the corresponding IP address for the requested domain.

2. **Recursive Query**: If the IP address is not cached, the request is sent to a DNS resolver, which may query various DNS servers to resolve the name.

3. **Root Name Servers**: The resolver starts by asking the root name servers, which direct it to the appropriate Top-Level Domain (TLD) servers associated with the domain (e.g., .com, .org).

4. **TLD Name Servers**: The TLD servers then provide the address of the authoritative DNS servers for the specific domain.

5. **Authoritative Name Servers**: Finally, the authoritative servers respond with the IP address that corresponds to the requested domain name.

4.4.2 Types of DNS Records

Several types of DNS records exist to provide various functionalities:

- **A Record**: Maps a domain name to an

IPv4 address.

- **AAAA Record**: Maps a domain name to an IPv6 address.

- **CNAME Record**: Provides an alias for an existing A record.

- **MX Record**: Specifies mail exchange servers associated with the domain.

- **NS Record**: Indicates which DNS servers are authoritative for a domain.

4.4.3 DNS Caching

DNS responses can be cached by both the resolver and the client's system to improve efficiency and reduce the load on DNS servers. This caching mechanism means that subsequent requests for the same domain can be resolved faster, as the IP is pulled from the cache instead of going through the resolution process again.

4.4.4 Security Considerations

Despite its critical role in networking, DNS is not immune to security threats. Vulnerabilities, such as DNS spoofing and cache poisoning, can lead to malicious rerouting of traffic or unauthorized access to sensitive information.

To mitigate these threats, measures such as DNSSEC (Domain Name System Security Extensions) have been introduced, providing an added layer of security by allowing the verification of responses and ensuring that the information received is legitimate.

In this chapter, we have explored the key protocols and configuration methods that form the backbone of modern networking. From the principles of IP addressing to the specifics of DHCP and the vital role of DNS, understanding these components is essential for effectively managing and configuring networks. As technology continues to evolve, so too will the methods by which we connect and communicate across the digital landscape, but the fundamental principles outlined in this chapter will remain relevant to networking professionals for years to come.

Chapter 5: Network Security

Network security is a crucial aspect of information technology, essential for protecting both the data and the integrity of networks from various threats. As technology evolves, the complexity and sophistication of these threats increase, making it imperative for organizations to implement robust security measures. This chapter will explore the various dimensions of network security, covering the types of threats encountered, protective mechanisms such as firewalls, intrusion detection systems (IDS), virtual private networks (VPNs), and the essential role of encryption and authentication.

5.1 Threats to Security

Various types of network security threats can compromise the integrity, confidentiality, and availability of information systems. Understanding these threats is the first step towards effective management and mitigation.

5.1.1 Malware

Malware is a broad category that encompasses various malicious software designed to harm, exploit, or otherwise compromise networks. Common types of malware include viruses, worms, Trojan horses, ransomware, and spyware. Each type has its unique characteristics:

- **Viruses** replicate themselves by inserting copies into other programs, files, or the boot sector of the hard drive.

- **Worms** are similar but can spread independently without user intervention, often exploiting vulnerabilities in software or operating systems.

- **Trojan horses** disguise themselves as legitimate software to trick users into executing them.

- **Ransomware** encrypts files and

demands a ransom for decryption, causing significant data loss and downtime.

- **Spyware** monitors user activity, capturing sensitive information such as passwords and credit card numbers.

5.1.2 Phishing Attacks

Phishing attacks employ social engineering tactics to deceive users into revealing sensitive information or downloading malware. Attackers often impersonate trusted entities via email or fake websites, prompting users to enter personal or financial details. Variants include:

- **Spear Phishing**, which targets specific individuals or organizations.

- **Whaling**, aimed at high-profile targets such as executives.

- **Vishing**, which involves voice calls or messages to carry out scams.

5.1.3 Denial of Service (DoS) Attacks

Denial of Service attacks aim to disrupt the services of a host connected to the internet by overwhelming it with traffic, rendering it unavailable to legitimate users. Distributed Denial of Service (DDoS) attacks deploy multiple compromised systems to launch a coordinated attack, significantly increasing their effectiveness.

5.1.4 Man-in-the-Middle (MitM) Attacks

In MitM attacks, an adversary intercepts and potentially alters the communication between two parties without their knowledge. This can occur over unsecured networks, particularly in public Wi-Fi settings. By eavesdropping, attackers can capture sensitive data and even inject malicious code into the communications.

5.1.5 Insider Threats

While external threats receive much focus, insiders, including employees or contractors, can pose significant risks. These threats can be intentional, such as data theft or sabotage, or unintentional due to negligence or lack of awareness regarding security policies.

5.1.6 Advanced Persistent Threats (APTs)

APTs are long-term targeted attacks aimed at stealing sensitive information over an extended period. Typically carried out by well-funded and skilled adversaries, APTs employ multiple attack vectors to breach networks, maintaining a low profile to avoid detection while exfiltrating data.

5.2 Firewalls and Protection Systems

Firewalls serve as essential barriers between trusted and untrusted networks. They determine which traffic is allowed or blocked based on predetermined security rules and policies.

5.2.1 Types of Firewalls

- **Packet Filtering Firewalls**: These operate at the network layer, inspecting packets and allowing or blocking them based solely on IP address, port number, and protocol. They are fast and efficient but offer limited security.

- **Stateful Inspection Firewalls**: These keep track of the state of active connections and make decisions based on the context of traffic, making them more secure than simple packet filtering. They can understand and differentiate between legitimate and malicious data packets.

- **Application Layer Firewalls**: Operating at the application layer, these firewalls can inspect traffic based on the application and enforce security policies at the HTTP layer. This type includes web application firewalls (WAFs), which protect applications by filtering and monitoring HTTP traffic.

- **Next-Generation Firewalls (NGFW)**: These combine traditional firewall capabilities with advanced features such as intrusion prevention systems (IPS), deep packet inspection, and application awareness, providing comprehensive security and more dynamic control.

5.2.2 Unified Threat Management (UTM)

Unified Threat Management systems are integrated solutions that combine multiple security features, including firewalls, antivirus, intrusion detection, and more. UTMs provide a single point of management for security, making it easier for organizations to monitor and respond to threats.

5.2.3 Configuration and Policy Management

Proper configuration of firewalls and security policies is paramount. Organizations should regularly review access rules, implement the principle of least privilege, and perform scheduled audits to ensure compliance with security protocols.

5.3 Intrusion Detection Systems (IDS)

Intrusion Detection Systems monitor network traffic for suspicious activity and potential threats. They can be classified into two main types:

5.3.1 Network-Based Intrusion Detection Systems (NIDS)

NIDS monitors the traffic on a network segment, analyzing incoming and outgoing packets for patterns that may indicate malicious activity. This type of system is particularly effective in identifying Denial-of-Service attacks and unauthorized access attempts.

5.3.2 Host-Based Intrusion Detection Systems (HIDS)

HIDS operates on individual hosts or endpoints, monitoring system calls, file modifications, and application activity. This type of IDS can detect unauthorized file changes or malicious behavior by monitoring the endpoint's internal activities.

5.3.3 Signature-Based Detection

Signature-based detection involves looking for known patterns of malware or attack vectors. This method is effective for identifying recognized threats but may struggle against new or polymorphic threats that do not have discernible signatures.

5.3.4 Anomaly-Based Detection

Anomaly-based detection establishes a baseline of normal behavior and identifies deviations from this baseline. By highlighting unusual network traffic patterns or system behaviors, it can identify new, previously unknown threats but may also yield false positives.

5.3.5 Intrusion Prevention Systems (IPS)

IPS builds on the work of IDS but goes a step

further by actively blocking detected threats in real time. This capacity requires the IPS to not only identify and alert but also take action to mitigate identified threats immediately.

5.4 Virtual Private Network (VPN)

Virtual Private Networks provide a secure connection over a public or insecure network. They achieve this by creating encrypted tunnels between the user's device and the VPN server.

5.4.1 Benefits of VPNs

- **Enhanced Security**: VPNs encrypt data in transit, making it difficult for unauthorized users or attackers to access or decipher the communication.

- **Anonymity and Privacy**: By masking the user's IP address and routing traffic through the VPN server, VPNs enhance anonymity and privacy, protecting users from tracking and surveillance.

- **Remote Access**: VPNs enable secure remote access to corporate networks, allowing employees to connect safely from various locations without compromising network security.

5.4.2 VPN Protocols

Various protocols govern how data is transmitted over VPNs, including:

- **OpenVPN**: An open-source protocol known for its strong security and flexibility.

- **IPsec**: A suite of protocols that encrypts data at the IP level, commonly used in combination with L2TP (Layer 2 Tunneling Protocol).

- **L2TP**: Often used with IPsec to provide increased security.

- **IKEv2**: Known for speed and security, it's particularly effective for mobile devices.

5.5 Encryption and Authentication

Encryption and authentication are foundational components of network security, ensuring that data is not only protected from unauthorized access but also that it is transmitted securely.

5.5.1 Encryption

Encryption transforms readable data into an unreadable format, reversible only with the appropriate decryption key. There are two primary types of encryption:

- **Symmetric Encryption**: The same key is used for both encryption and decryption. While it is faster, key distribution and management can pose challenges.

- **Asymmetric Encryption**: Uses a pair of keys, a public key for encryption and a private key for decryption. This approach enhances security but can be slower than symmetric methods.

5.5.2 Importance of Encryption Protocols

Protocols such as SSL/TLS (Secure Sockets Layer/Transport Layer Security) protect data in transit, widely used for securing web communications. VPN protocols often incorporate encryption to ensure secure connections over the internet.

5.5.3 Authentication Mechanisms

Authentication verifies users' identities before granting access to networks or systems. Common methods include:

- **Password-Based Authentication**: While ubiquitous, it can be vulnerable to attacks if users choose weak passwords or if passwords are compromised through phishing attempts.

- **Two-Factor Authentication (2FA)**: This method combines two forms of authentication, typically something a user knows (like a password) and something the user has (like a smartphone app or hardware token), significantly enhancing security.

- **Biometric Authentication**: Uses physical characteristics, such as fingerprints or facial recognition, to authenticate users, offering a more secure alternative to traditional methods.

5.5.4 Identity and Access Management (IAM)

IAM frameworks govern the processes, policies, and technologies enabling organizations to manage user identities and regulate access to critical resources. Best practices include implementing least privilege access, regularly reviewing user permissions, and ensuring proper onboarding and offboarding processes for employees.

In summary, network security is a multidimensional field that requires continuous monitoring, updated technology, and rigorous policies to combat ever-evolving threats. The interplay between understanding potential threats and implementing a robust security architecture, including firewalls, IDS, VPNs, and encryption, is essential for maintaining the integrity, confidentiality, and availability of data. As technology continues to advance, organizations must remain vigilant, adaptable, and proactive in their cybersecurity strategies to protect against new and emerging risks.

Chapter 6: Network Monitoring and Maintenance

In today's digital era, the efficacy of a network significantly determines the overall productivity of an organization. From enabling seamless communication to supporting critical applications, a well-maintained and monitored network is paramount. In this chapter, we will delve into several aspects of network monitoring and maintenance, including essential tools, performance optimization strategies, preventive and corrective maintenance practices, and the importance of backing up network configurations.

6.1 Monitoring Tools

6.1.1 Importance of Monitoring Tools

Monitoring tools play a crucial role in

maintaining the health and efficiency of a network. These tools provide real-time data about network performance, identify potential issues before they impact operations, and enable network administrators to make informed decisions about resource allocation and network enhancements.

6.1.2 Types of Monitoring Tools

There are several types of monitoring tools available, each designed for specific functions within the network management spectrum.

a. Network Performance Monitors (NPM)

NPM tools focus primarily on monitoring the performance metrics of network devices. They can measure bandwidth usage, latency, packet loss, and other vital statistics. Some notable NPM tools include SolarWinds Network

Performance Monitor, PRTG Network Monitor, and Nagios.

b. Network Configuration Managers (NCM)

These tools help in managing and monitoring the configurations of various network devices. NCM tools can track changes in configurations, alert administrators about unauthorized changes, and facilitate the rollback to previous states when necessary. Examples include SolarWinds Network Configuration Manager and ManageEngine Network Configuration Manager.

c. Security Information and Event Management (SIEM)

SIEM tools provide comprehensive security monitoring by collecting and analyzing security data from across the network. These tools help in detecting and responding to security incidents in real-time. Popular SIEM tools are Splunk, IBM QRadar, and ArcSight.

d. Application Performance Monitoring (APM)

APM tools focus on the performance of applications that run over the network. They help ensure that applications are operating efficiently and that any bottlenecks or issues affecting application performance are quickly identified. Examples include New Relic and Datadog.

6.1.3 Integration of Tools

Integrating multiple monitoring tools into a cohesive dashboard allows network administrators to gain a holistic view of the network. For instance, tying together performance and security monitoring can help identify how performance issues may relate to security events. Modern software solutions often feature APIs and plugins to support the integration of various tools, enhancing their overall capability.

6.2 Network Performance and Optimization

6.2.1 Performance Metrics

To optimize network performance effectively, it is essential to understand and monitor various performance metrics, including:

- **Bandwidth Utilization:** Measures how much of the available bandwidth is being used, indicating the network's capacity and identifying potential congestion points.

- **Latency:** Assesses the time it takes for

data packets to travel from the source to the destination. High latency can lead to slow application performance.

- **Packet Loss:** Indicates the percentage of packets that fail to reach their destination, which can degrade user experience significantly.

- **Jitter:** Measures the variation in packet arrival times, which can affect real-time communications like voice over IP (VoIP) and video conferencing.

6.2.2 Optimization Techniques

Once key performance metrics have been established, several optimization techniques can enhance network performance:

a. Traffic Shaping

Traffic shaping involves managing bandwidth allocation for different types of network traffic to ensure that critical applications receive the necessary resources. By prioritizing traffic, organizations can minimize latency and packet loss for high-priority applications.

b. Load Balancing

Load balancing distributes workloads across multiple resources to ensure no single device or link becomes a bottleneck. This can improve the speed and reliability of applications, enhancing overall user experience.

c. Quality of Service (QoS)

Implementing QoS policies allows network

administrators to control which types of traffic take precedence over others. For instance, prioritizing VoIP traffic can ensure clearer calls even during periods of high network utilization.

d. Regular Performance Reviews

Conducting regular performance reviews can help in identifying degradation patterns and taking timely actions to mitigate them. Utilizing dashboards provided by monitoring tools enables administrators to visualize data trends over time.

6.3 Preventive and Corrective Maintenance

6.3.1 Preventive Maintenance

Preventive maintenance involves scheduled checks and updates to prevent network issues before they occur. This proactive approach ensures that network devices remain in good working order, mitigating downtime and potential data loss.

a. Regular Firmware and Software Updates

Keeping device firmware and software up to date is essential for network security and performance. Updates often include patches for security vulnerabilities and performance enhancements.

b. Component Inspection

Regularly inspecting network hardware components for wear and tear can avoid unexpected failures. Checking for overheating, loose connections, and environmental factors (like humidity and dust) can prolong the lifespan of network devices.

c. Documentation and Change Management

Maintaining accurate documentation of network configurations, changes, and maintenance activities ensures that administrators have a clear picture of the network's evolution. This documentation aids in troubleshooting and can streamline recovery efforts in case of unexpected failures.

6.3.2 Corrective Maintenance

Despite best efforts, issues may still occur, necessitating corrective maintenance. This involves responding to and fixing issues as they arise.

a. Incident Response Plan

Having a well-defined incident response plan can drastically reduce the time to resolution when problems occur. This plan should outline the steps to take when different types of network issues arise.

b. Troubleshooting Protocols

Establishing standardized troubleshooting protocols ensures that network issues are diagnosed and resolved efficiently. Each network team member should be trained on these protocols to enable a swift response.

c. Post-Issue Analysis

Once an issue has been resolved, conducting a post-issue analysis can provide valuable insights into the root causes. This process can inform future preventive measures and adjustments to maintenance practices.

6.4 Backup of Network Configuration

6.4.1 Importance of Backing Up Network Configurations

Backing up network configuration files is a fundamental practice that safeguards against data loss due to hardware failure, misconfiguration, or cyberattacks. Configuration backups allow organizations to restore network devices to their previous operational states quickly.

6.4.2 Backup Strategies

a. Automated Backups

Implementing automated backup solutions ensures that configurations are regularly saved without manual intervention. Many configuration management tools offer scheduled backups that occur daily, weekly, or monthly, depending on the organization's needs.

b. Version Control

Maintaining version control for backups allows network administrators to track changes over time. This practice enables organizations to revert to previous configurations if a new deployment introduces issues.

c. Offsite Storage

To safeguard against local failures or disasters, backing up configurations to offsite locations or cloud storage is advisable. This adds an extra layer of protection and promotes business continuity.

6.4.3 Regular Review and Testing of Backups

Regularly reviewing and testing backups ensures that they remain viable and can be restored without issues. Periodic drills where network configurations are restored in a controlled environment can help identify any potential gaps in the backup process.

By comprehensively monitoring network performance and establishing rigorous maintenance processes, organizations can enhance reliability, prevent issues, and secure their network infrastructure. Through effective utilization of monitoring tools, optimization techniques, and a solid backup strategy, network administrators can ensure their networks are secure, efficient, and capable of meeting the evolving demands of today's digital landscape.

Chapter 7: Troubleshooting

In the field of technology and network management, troubleshooting is an essential skill. It involves diagnosing and resolving issues that arise in systems, networks, and devices. Effective troubleshooting incorporates a systematic approach, which allows professionals and users alike to efficiently identify problems and find solutions. This chapter will delve into various aspects of troubleshooting, including techniques, tools, and common issues encountered in networking environments.

7.1 Troubleshooting Techniques

Troubleshooting can be defined as a methodical process for diagnosing faults within a system or network. It typically follows a structured approach that includes several key steps: identifying the problem, isolating the cause, testing potential solutions, and verifying that the issue has been resolved. Here, we will discuss several established troubleshooting techniques.

7.1.1 The Basic Troubleshooting Methodology

The basic troubleshooting methodology consists of the following steps:

1. **Identification of the Problem**: Clearly define the issue by gathering information from users or system logs. What are the symptoms? When did the problem occur? Understanding the context can provide valuable insight into the root cause.

2. **Establishing a Theory of Probable Cause**: Formulate hypotheses about potential causes of the problem based on the symptoms and context. Consider common failures related to the hardware, software,

configuration, and network.

3. **Testing the Theory**: Implement tests to confirm or disprove your theories. This may involve changing configurations, replacing components, or running diagnostic tools.

4. **Establishing a Plan of Action**: Once the theory is confirmed, outline a step-by-step approach to resolve the issue. Ensure that the planned solution does not disrupt other parts of the system.

5. **Implementing the Solution**: Carry out your plan methodically. Ensure that changes are documented and that there's a contingency plan in place, in case the solution causes additional problems.

6. **Verifying Functionality**: After implementing the solution, verify that the issue is resolved. Perform comprehensive tests

to confirm that the system is functioning as expected.

7. **Documentation**: Regardless of the outcome, document what was learned during the troubleshooting process. This could be helpful for future reference and assists in building a knowledge base.

7.1.2 The 80/20 Rule

In troubleshooting, the 80/20 rule (or Pareto Principle) often applies. It suggests that 80% of problems can typically be traced back to 20% of the potential causes. By focusing on these common causes rather than exploring every possibility, you can streamline the troubleshooting process. Train your awareness to recognize patterns in failures, particularly in environments where certain types of equipment or configurations are predominate.

7.1.3 Divide and Conquer

This technique involves breaking down a large system into smaller components in order to isolate the issue. By systematically testing each section, you can pinpoint the failure more quickly. Start from a known good state (a "baseline") and progressively reintroduce changes or components until the problem reappears.

7.1.4 The Five Whys

A simple but effective technique is the "Five Whys." When faced with a problem, keep asking "why" until you reach the root cause. This method encourages deep reasoning about problems and helps prevent superficial solutions.

7.1.5 Root Cause Analysis

This method focuses on identifying underlying reasons for failures. A variety of techniques, such as Fishbone Diagrams, help visualize cause-and-effect relationships, ultimately leading to the root cause. By addressing the root cause, you can prevent recurrence and enhance overall system stability and performance.

7.2 Tools for Troubleshooting

Having the right tools at your disposal is imperative for effective troubleshooting. These tools can assist in diagnosing problems, monitoring systems, and analyzing performance. Here are some essential categories and examples of troubleshooting tools:

7.2.1 Network Monitoring Tools

Network monitoring tools can track network traffic, performance metrics, and device statuses. This vital information helps pinpoint problems before they escalate.

- **Wireshark**: A free, open-source packet analyzer that provides detailed information about network traffic and protocols. Wireshark is invaluable for deep packet analysis.

- **Nagios**: A powerful monitoring system that enables you to monitor systems, networks, and infrastructure for issues. It can alert administrators when problems arise.

- **SolarWinds Network Performance Monitor**: A commercial solution that provides insights into network performance, issues, and trends. It offers user-friendly dashboards and reporting features.

7.2.2 Diagnostic Tools

Various diagnostic tools can assist in troubleshooting hardware and software failures.

- **Ping and Traceroute**: Basic yet fundamental networking commands used to check connectivity and discover routing paths. They are essential for identifying where connections fail.

- **IP Config/IF Config**: Command-line utilities for displaying and configuring network interface settings on Windows (ipconfig) and Linux/Unix systems (ifconfig).

- **Event Viewer**: Integrated into Windows systems, it logs events such as warnings and errors. Reviewing logs can help identify software and system failures.

7.2.3 Remote Access Tools

Remote access tools allow technicians to remediate issues without being physically present.

- **TeamViewer**: A widely-used remote access and support tool that enables users to connect and control devices remotely.

- **Remote Desktop Protocol (RDP)**: A built-in feature on Windows that facilitates remote network administration and troubleshooting.

7.2.4 Performance and Load Testing Tools

Performance testing tools evaluate how systems behave under stress, allowing for better anticipation of possible issues before they arise.

- **Apache JMeter**: An open-source tool primarily used for load testing web applications. It is useful for simulating user behavior to identify how systems perform under different loads.

- **LoadRunner**: A commercial load testing tool that allows you to test and assess the performance of applications under load.

7.2.5 Configuration Management Tools

Configuration management tools ensure that systems are correctly configured and maintained over time.

- **Ansible**: An open-source automation tool that helps manage configurations and deployments across multiple systems efficiently.

- **Puppet**: Another configuration management tool that automates the provisioning and configuration of physical and virtual servers.

7.3 Common Network Issues and Solutions

Countless issues can arise within a network, but certain problems tend to be particularly frequent. Understanding the common problems and their resolutions can expedite troubleshooting and minimize downtime.

7.3.1 Connectivity Issues

Symptoms:

Users report that they cannot connect to the internet or access specific resources.

Solutions:

- **Ensure Connection**: Check if all cables are properly connected, including network cables and power supplies for switches and routers. Validate that devices are powered on.

- **Restart Devices**: A simple restart of the affected devices (modem, router, switch, or computer) can eliminate temporary glitches.

- **Check IP Configuration**: Use the `ipconfig` command on Windows or `ifconfig` on Linux to ensure that the device has a valid IP address. If not, consider releasing and renewing the IP address.

- **DNS Issues**: If users can reach certain sites but not others, investigate DNS settings. Clearing the DNS cache with the `ipconfig

/flushdns` command may be necessary.

7.3.2 Slow Network Performance

Symptoms:

Users experience sluggish speeds when accessing resources or the internet.

Solutions:

- **Check Bandwidth Usage**: Monitor network traffic using tools like Wireshark or dedicated monitoring solutions to identify bandwidth hogs. Things like large uploads or streaming services may be affecting performance.

- **Network Congestion**: Investigate the network topology to determine if congestion during peak hours is contributing to slow speeds. Load balancing and quality-of-service configurations may be necessary.

- **Hardware Limitations**: Inspect the capacity of routers and switches. Replacing outdated hardware with larger capacity devices may improve performance.

7.3.3 Wireless Issues

Symptoms:

Users cannot connect to the Wi-Fi network or experience frequent disconnections.

Solutions:

- **Distance from Access Points**: Ensure that users are within an acceptable range of wireless access points, as excessive distance can cause instability.

- **Interference**: Evaluate the network for interference from other electronic devices (e.g., microwaves, cordless phones) and neighboring networks. Changing the Wi-Fi channel or frequency band can sometimes alleviate interference issues.

- **Firmware Updates**: Ensure that all wireless devices are updated with the latest firmware patches to fix known issues.

7.3.4 Security Breaches

Symptoms:

Unexpected traffic, unauthorized access, or altered configurations may suggest a security breach.

Solutions:

- **Implement Firewalls**: Make use of firewalls to restrict unauthorized access and monitor incoming and outgoing traffic.

- **Update Security Protocols**: Ensure that all devices have the latest security patches installed. Use strong authentication methods and regularly change passwords.

- **Network Segmentation**: Segment your network into different sections to limit the lateral movement of potential attackers. Isolate critical devices and sensitive data.

Troubleshooting is an intricate dance of problem identification, hypothesis testing, implementation, and verification. It requires not only a systematic approach but also a deep understanding of systems and networks. In this chapter, we have explored various troubleshooting techniques, essential tools, and common network issues along with their solutions. As technology continues to evolve, so too will the challenges and techniques in troubleshooting, necessitating an ongoing commitment to learning and adaptation.

By mastering these methods and utilizing the right tools, both individuals and organizations can minimize downtime and enhance overall system performance. Ultimately, effective troubleshooting not only saves time but also enhances the reliability of technology systems in an increasingly interconnected world.

Chapter 8: Virtualization and Cloud Networking

8.1 Introduction to Virtualization

Virtualization is a technology that enables a single physical machine to run multiple operating systems and applications concurrently, effectively carving up resources and maximizing hardware utilization. In essence, virtualization abstracts physical hardware, creating a virtual layer that allows multiple operating systems to exist on a single server as virtual machines (VMs). This separation between hardware and software has transformed the IT landscape, enabling businesses to achieve higher efficiency, agility, and flexibility.

Types of Virtualization

There are several types of virtualization, each

serving different purposes and offering various benefits:

1. **Server Virtualization:** This is the most common form, where physical servers are transformed into several virtual servers. This allows businesses to consolidate workloads, maximize resource usage, and simplify management.

2. **Desktop Virtualization:** This allows users to run various desktop environments on a single centralized server. It is beneficial for organizations looking to manage desktop environments efficiently, particularly in remote work scenarios.

3. **Application Virtualization:** This separates applications from the underlying operating system, allowing them to run without installation on a local machine. This facilitates easier application deployment and management.

4. **Network Virtualization:** This abstracts physical networking resources, allowing multiple virtual networks to coexist on a single physical network. Each virtual network can have its own policies and configurations, providing flexibility and maximized resource use.

5. **Storage Virtualization:** This combines physical storage devices to create a single logical storage unit, enhancing storage management, scalability, and availability.

With virtualization, organizations can enhance their disaster recovery capabilities, reduce hardware costs, and simplify system administration. As the cloud continues to evolve, the importance of virtualization becomes even more critical, forming the backbone of cloud computing infrastructure.

8.2 Virtual Networks

Virtual networks are a core concept in modern networking that allow for the creation of logical networks independent of the physical hardware. They provide the agility and flexibility needed for cloud computing and virtualized environments, enabling organizations to dynamically provision, configure, and manage network resources.

Components of Virtual Networks

1. **Virtual LANs (VLANs):** VLANs segment a single physical network into multiple logical networks. Devices in the same VLAN can communicate with each other regardless of their physical location, enhancing security and reducing broadcast traffic.

2. **Overlay Networks:** These networks

operate over existing physical networks and can provide additional network functionality such as encapsulation and tunneling. Technologies like VXLAN (Virtual Extensible LAN) are used to create overlay networks, which enable vast scalability and isolation.

3. **Network Functions Virtualization (NFV):** NFV allows network services to be virtualized and run on general-purpose hardware instead of proprietary hardware appliances. This reduces capital expenditures and allows for the rapid deployment of new services.

4. **Software-Defined Networking (SDN):** SDN separates the control plane from the data plane in networking, allowing for centralized management of the network through software applications. This flexibility enables dynamic changes based on traffic demands and service requirements.

Benefits of Virtual Networks

Virtual networks offer numerous advantages, including:

- **Enhanced Network Security:** By isolating sensitive applications and data into distinct virtual networks, organizations can minimize risks and contain potential security breaches.

- **Scalability:** Virtual networks can easily scale up or down based on demand, enabling organizations to respond to changing business needs without the need for extensive hardware investments.

- **Cost Efficiency:** By consolidating resources and reducing hardware requirements, virtual networks can decrease operational costs associated with network management and maintenance.

- **Improved Resource Utilization:** Virtual networks enable organizations to maximize their use of physical network equipment, leading to efficiency gains and reduced waste.

8.3 Cloud Computing and Networking

Cloud computing refers to the delivery of on-demand computing resources, such as servers, storage, databases, networking, software, and analytics, over the Internet. This technology has reshaped how organizations consume IT resources and manage their digital operations.

The Role of Networking in Cloud Computing

Networking is a fundamental component of

cloud computing. It facilitates communication between cloud resources, end-users, and various services. With the rise of cloud computing, the networking infrastructure also had to evolve, which led to the development of new networking paradigms.

1. **Public vs. Private Cloud Networking:** In public clouds, resources are shared among multiple users, whereas private clouds are dedicated to a single organization. Each model has unique networking considerations in terms of architecture, security, and management.

2. **Hybrid Cloud Networking:** A combination of public and private clouds, hybrid cloud environments require robust networking solutions to ensure seamless communication between different environments. This is often achieved through virtual private networks (VPNs) and dedicated connections.

3. **Multicloud Networking:** As organizations adopt services from multiple cloud providers, managing networking effectively across these environments presents challenges. Solutions such as cloud routers and interconnects help facilitate communication and data transfer.

Challenges in Cloud Networking

While cloud computing offers numerous benefits, it also presents networking challenges:

- **Latency and Bandwidth Issues:** Depending on user location and network conditions, data transmission to and from cloud environments may experience limitations in latency and bandwidth. Tools that optimize network performance are crucial.

- **Security Concerns:** Transmitting sensitive data over the internet necessitates robust security measures, such as encryption, firewalls, and secure access controls, to protect data from unauthorized access and breaches.

- **Configuring Networks for Cloud Operations:** Ensuring that networks are properly configured to support fluctuating workloads and dynamic provisioning requires careful planning and management.

Future of Cloud Networking

As organizations increasingly migrate to cloud environments, the future of cloud networking looks promising. Innovations such as edge computing, further use of AI and machine learning for network management, and the growth of 5G technology will enhance the capabilities and performance of cloud networks.

8.4 IaaS, PaaS, and SaaS

The cloud computing landscape consists of several service models, with the three most prominent being Infrastructure as a Service (IaaS), Platform as a Service (PaaS), and Software as a Service (SaaS). Each service model offers different levels of control and management capabilities, catering to various organizational needs.

Infrastructure as a Service (IaaS)

IaaS provides virtualized computing resources over the Internet. It allows businesses to rent IT infrastructure, such as servers, storage, and networking, on a pay-as-you-go basis. This model offers organizations flexibility and scalability based on their operational requirements.

Key Features of IaaS:

- **Scalability:** Organizations can quickly scale up or down their infrastructure resources, responding to changing workload demands without upfront investments.

- **Cost-Effectiveness:** With IaaS, companies pay only for the resources they use, reducing capital expenses associated with purchasing hardware.

- **Control:** Organizations maintain control over their infrastructure, allowing for custom configurations and management of virtualized environments.

Use Cases for IaaS:

- Hosting websites and applications

- Development and testing environments

- Data storage and backup solutions

Platform as a Service (PaaS)

PaaS provides a platform that allows developers to build, deploy, and manage applications without needing to manage underlying infrastructure. This model is tailored for software development and focuses on providing tools and services that facilitate rapid application development.

Key Features of PaaS:

- **Development Tools:** PaaS offerings often include development frameworks, databases, and middleware that streamline the application development process.

- **Multi-tenant Architecture:** PaaS platforms typically have a multi-tenant architecture, allowing multiple users to share the same application resources while keeping their data isolated.

- **Integrated Environment:** PaaS combines various services and tools into a cohesive environment, eliminating the complexities of integrating different components.

Use Cases for PaaS:

- Application development and deployment

- API development

- Integration of data across various sources

Software as a Service (SaaS)

SaaS is a software distribution model where

applications are hosted in the cloud and made available to users over the Internet. Users can access SaaS applications through a web browser without needing to install or maintain the software on their devices.

Key Features of SaaS:

- **Accessibility:** SaaS applications are accessible from any device with an Internet connection, facilitating remote work and collaboration.

- **Automatic Updates:** SaaS providers handle software updates, ensuring users always have access to the latest features and security patches.

- **Subscription-Based Pricing:** SaaS typically follows a subscription model, allowing businesses to manage costs easily and predict expenses.

Use Cases for SaaS:

- Customer relationship management (CRM)

- Email and collaboration tools (e.g., Microsoft 365, Google Workspace)

- Accounting and financial software (e.g., QuickBooks Online)

Summary

Understanding the various aspects of virtualization and cloud networking is essential for modern organizations seeking to leverage technology for business growth. By utilizing virtualization technologies, businesses can optimize their resources, enhance security, and improve scalability. Cloud networking complements these strategies by offering flexible communication and infrastructure solutions that adapt to the evolving technological landscape. Finally, the service models of IaaS, PaaS, and SaaS provide a structured way for organizations to consume IT resources based on their specific needs, driving innovation and efficiency in their operations. As organizations continue to adopt these technologies, they will be better equipped to navigate the complexities of digital transformation and the demands of the modern business environment.

Chapter 9: Future Trends in Networking

As we stand on the brink of rapid technological advancement, the domain of networking is poised to undergo significant transformations. This chapter delves into key trends that are shaping the future of network administration, focusing on 5G, the Internet of Things (IoT), Software-Defined Networking (SDN), and the increasing application of Artificial Intelligence (AI) in networking.

9.1 5G Networks

The rollout of 5G networks marks a pivotal moment in the evolution of telecommunications. Characterized by ultra-high-speed data transmission, low latency, and the ability to connect a vast number of devices concurrently, 5G technology is set to revolutionize how networks operate and serve their users.

Key Features of 5G Networks:

- **Ultra-Reliable Low Latency Communication (URLLC):** 5G enables communication with latencies as low as one millisecond, making it ideal for applications requiring immediate feedback, such as autonomous vehicles and remote surgeries.

- **Massive Machine-Type Communication (mMTC):** 5G can support a projected one million devices per square kilometer, perfect for smart cities and the expansion of IoT devices.

- **Enhanced Mobile Broadband (eMBB):** With speeds up to 20 Gbps, 5G substantially improves the user experience for mobile broadband services, including high-definition streaming and virtual reality applications.

Implications for Network Administration:

The implementation of 5G drives the need for advanced network management strategies. Administrators must adapt to the increased complexity of the network; they will need to ensure network reliability and security while managing the explosive growth in device connectivity.

Moreover, as carriers pivot to 5G, they are revisiting their infrastructure investments. Network admins will play a crucial role in integrating legacy technologies with new 5G systems. This includes troubleshooting and maintaining older hardware while supporting dynamic, software-driven 5G components.

Impact on Other Technologies:

5G is expected to enhance the functioning of

various technologies, including augmented reality (AR) and virtual reality (VR), making remote collaboration more feasible and effective than ever. Enhanced data rates and lower latency will provide seamless interaction in virtual environments, paving the way for industries to rethink how they train employees, showcase products, and engage with customers.

9.2 Internet of Things (IoT)

The Internet of Things represents a paradigm shift in networking, where everyday devices become interconnected and can communicate with one another. Consisting of an array of devices, from smart home appliances to industrial sensors, IoT extends the reach of the internet beyond traditional computing devices.

Growth and Security Concerns:

With predictions suggesting that there could be more than 50 billion connected IoT devices by 2030, network administrators must prioritize security and scalability. Each IoT device presents a potential vulnerability. Network admins are tasked with implementing robust security measures, such as end-to-end encryption and secure access protocols, to protect sensitive data transferred through these devices.

Moreover, scalability becomes a crucial consideration as the number of devices grows exponentially. Administrators must ensure the network infrastructure is capable of handling the increased load without compromising performance or security.

Data Management and Analytics:

IoT devices generate massive amounts of data. Network administrators need to implement strategies for data collection, storage, and analysis. The ability to glean insights from this data will drive better decision-making processes in industries ranging from healthcare to transportation.

Real-time analytics will allow organizations to react quickly to changing conditions, thereby improving operational efficiency. Network administrators should consider implementing edge computing solutions to process data closer to where it is generated, reducing latency, and bandwidth consumption while providing more timely insights.

9.3 Software-Defined Networking (SDN)

Software-Defined Networking (SDN) is transforming how networks are designed and managed. By decoupling the control plane from the data plane, SDN allows for more agility and innovation in network management.

Key Benefits of SDN:

- **Centralized Control:** Through a centralized controller, administrators can manage network resources dynamically. This leads to improved visibility and control over the entire network infrastructure.

- **Automation and Orchestration:** SDN simplifies provisioning and management through automation tools. Administrators can automate routine tasks, reducing the time and effort involved in network management.

- **Enhanced Flexibility:** Changes to the network can be made quickly in response to real-time demand. Network admins can create, modify, and delete network services on-the-fly, making it easier to align resources with changing business strategies.

Integration with 5G and IoT:

The synergy between SDN, 5G, and IoT is significant. As IoT devices proliferate and demand for low-latency connections grows, SDN will help manage the complexities. For instance, through SDN, network admins can dynamically allocate bandwidth to different IoT devices based on their requirements.

As 5G networks adopt SDN principles, administrative overhead will decrease, while the network's overall reliability and performance improve. Network administrators must embrace SDN to remain competitive as these trends reshape the landscape.

9.4 Artificial Intelligence and Networking

Artificial Intelligence (AI) is beginning to play an influential role in various domains, including networking. As networks become more complex, utilizing AI can enhance performance, security, and management.

AI-Powered Network Management:

AI algorithms can analyze vast amounts of network data, identifying patterns and suggesting optimizations. The following applications highlight how AI can support network administration:

- **Predictive Analytics:** By analyzing historical performance data, AI can predict potential failures before they occur, enabling proactive maintenance and reducing downtime.

- **Anomaly Detection:** AI can detect unusual patterns in network traffic that may indicate a security breach or failure, prompting immediate intervention from network administrators.

- **Capacity Planning:** AI tools can assist in analyzing usage trends, helping network administrators to forecast future demands and adjust resource allocations accordingly.

Network Security Enhancements:

AI can enhance cybersecurity measures through intelligent threat detection systems that learn from network behavior. These systems can identify and mitigate threats more effectively than traditional methods.

For instance, machine learning algorithms can analyze behavioral patterns and automatically adapt security protocols in real-time, ensuring a stronger defense against evolving cyber threats.

Challenges of Implementing AI:

While AI offers numerous benefits, its implementation comes with challenges. Network administrators must ensure that they have the necessary data quality and quantity for AI algorithms to be effective. They also need to understand the ethical implications of using AI, including compliance with data protection regulations and algorithmic bias.

The trends explored in this chapter—5G, IoT, SDN, and AI—are not just technological advancements; they are transformative forces reshaping the networking landscape. As a network administrator, one must remain agile and adaptable, embracing these changes while focusing on security, scalability, and the effective management of resources. The future holds tremendous potential for network administration, promising innovations that will redefine connectivity and communication in the years to come.

Chapter 10: Technical Terms and Glossary for Network Administrators

As a network administrator, your role involves not only managing and maintaining network systems but also understanding a vast array of technical terms and concepts. This chapter aims to provide a comprehensive glossary of terms relevant to network administration, serving as both a reference guide for novice administrators and a refresher for seasoned professionals.

1. A

Access Control List (ACL): A set of rules that manages permissions for users or systems to access various resources within a network. ACLs help in enhancing security by defining who can connect, what resources they can access, and under what conditions.

Address Resolution Protocol (ARP): A network protocol used to find the hardware address (MAC address) of a host from its IP address. ARP operates mainly in IPv4 networks and is crucial for communication within local networks.

2. B

Bandwidth: The maximum rate of data transfer across a network path. It's measured in bits per second (bps) and directly affects the speed of data transmission in a network.

Bridge: A networking device that connects two or more network segments, enabling them to function as a single network. Bridges are used to reduce traffic by dividing collision domains.

3. C

Client-Server Model: A network architecture where multiple clients (devices or applications) request services, and a server provides those services. This model is foundational to most networking applications.

DHCP (Dynamic Host Configuration Protocol): A network management protocol that dynamically assigns IP addresses and provides other network configuration parameters to devices on a network, allowing them to communicate on an IP network.

4. D

Domain Name System (DNS): A hierarchical system that translates human-friendly domain names (like www.example.com) into IP addresses (like 192.0.2.1) that computers use to identify each other on the network.

Dynamic IP Address: An IP address that

is assigned to a device temporarily by a DHCP server. When the device disconnects, the IP address can be reused by other devices.

5. E

Ethernet: A widely used local area network (LAN) technology that defines a set of wiring and signaling standards for the physical and data link layers of the networking framework.

Extranet: A controlled private network that allows access to outsiders. Extranets are often used to share information with business partners or other external entities while maintaining security.

6. F

Firewall: A security device or software that monitors incoming and outgoing network traffic and decides whether to allow or block specific traffic based on predefined security rules.

FTP (File Transfer Protocol): A standard network protocol used to transfer files from one host to another over a TCP-based network such as the Internet. FTP can be used for transferring files both to and from a server.

7. G

Gateway: A network node used to connect two different networks, often with different protocols. Gateways typically serve as a "gate" between two networks, translating communication between them.

Group Policy: A feature in the Windows operating system that allows administrators to manage permissions and settings across multiple user accounts and computers within an Active Directory environment.

8. H

Honeypot: A security mechanism that creates a decoy system to lure attackers away from legitimate targets. Honeypots are used to detect, deflect, or study attempts to access a computer or network.

HTTP (Hypertext Transfer Protocol): The protocol used for transmitting hypertext via the World Wide Web. HTTP is the foundation of data communication on the web.

9. I

IP Address: A unique numerical label assigned to each device connected to a network that uses the Internet Protocol for communication. IP addresses can be either static (permanent) or dynamic (temporary).

ISP (Internet Service Provider): A company that provides individuals and organizations with access to the Internet. ISPs can offer various services, including broadband, DSL, cable, and fiber-optic connections.

10. J

Jitter: A variation in packet delay in a network, which can lead to uneven or choppy audio and video during transmissions. Jitter can be measured and mitigated through Quality of Service (QoS) techniques.

11. K

Kbps (Kilobits per second): A measure of data transfer speed equal to 1,000 bits per second. Kbps is commonly used to describe the speed of internet connections and data transmission/transfer rates.

12. L

LAN (Local Area Network): A network that connects computers and devices within a limited geographical area such as a building or campus. LANs are characterized by high data transfer rates and low latency.

Latency: The delay between a request for data and the actual receipt of that data. It's an important factor in network performance, especially for applications that require real-time communication.

13. M

MAC Address (Media Access Control Address): A unique identifier assigned to network interfaces for communications at the data link layer of a network. MAC addresses are used within a local network to identify devices.

Network Mask: Also known as a subnet mask, this defines the range of IP addresses that can be used within a particular subnet. It helps to determine the network and host portions of an IP address.

14. N

NAT (Network Address Translation): A method used in networks to map one IP address space into another by modifying network address information in the IP header of packets. NAT helps improve security and manage IP address usage.

Network Topology: The physical or logical arrangement of nodes in a network.

Common topologies include star, bus, ring, and mesh, each with its own advantages and disadvantages.

15. O

Open Systems Interconnection (OSI) Model: A conceptual framework used to understand and implement networking protocols in seven layers: Physical, Data Link, Network, Transport, Session, Presentation, and Application.

Outsourcing: The practice of delegating certain operations or responsibilities to a third party. In the context of network administration, this often means hiring external firms for network management tasks.

16. P

Packet: A formatted unit of data carried

by a packet-switched network. Each packet contains a header with routing information and the actual data being transmitted.

Ping: A network utility tool used to test the reachability of a host on an IP network. It sends ICMP echo request packets to the target host and measures the time it takes to receive a response.

17. Q

QoS (Quality of Service): A set of technologies that work on a network to manage bandwidth, prioritize traffic, and ensure a certain level of performance for critical applications.

Queue: In network terms, a queue is a mechanism for storing packets waiting to be processed or transmitted, which can help manage the flow of data across a network.

18. R

Router: A networking device that forwards packets between different networks, directing traffic based on routing tables and protocols. Routers operate at the Network layer (Layer 3) of the OSI model.

Subnetting: The practice of dividing a network into smaller, manageable sub-networks (subnets). Subnetting improves network performance and security by isolating groups of devices.

19. S

Switch: A networking device that connects multiple devices within a LAN and uses MAC addresses to forward data only to the intended recipient device. Switches operate at the Data Link layer (Layer 2) of the OSI model.

SSL (Secure Sockets Layer): A standard security protocol for establishing encrypted links between a web server and a browser, ensuring that all data passed between them remains private.

20. T

TCP/IP (Transmission Control Protocol/Internet Protocol): The fundamental suite of protocols that underpin the internet and enables different kinds of devices to communicate over various networks.

VLAN (Virtual Local Area Network): A subgroup within a LAN that defines a logical group of devices, creating a separate network that can communicate as if they are on the same physical network.

21. U

UDP (User Datagram Protocol): A communication protocol used across the internet that is less reliable than TCP but faster, as it does not require a connection to be established before data can be sent.

Uptime: The amount of time a system has been operational without any failures. High uptime is crucial for network services, as it reflects reliability and performance.

22. V

VPN (Virtual Private Network): A technology that creates a secure and encrypted connection over a less secure network, such as the Internet. VPNs enable remote users to connect to a private network securely.

VoIP (Voice over Internet Protocol): A technology that allows voice communication to take place over the Internet or a private network, converting voice into data packets for transmission.

23. W

WAN (Wide Area Network): A telecommunications network that extends over a large geographical area. WANs can connect multiple LANs and are often powered by leased telecommunication lines.

WLAN (Wireless Local Area Network): A LAN that uses wireless communication methods to connect devices, providing mobility and ease of access through technologies like Wi-Fi.

24. X

XSS (Cross-Site Scripting): A security vulnerability found in web applications that allows attackers to inject scripts into web pages viewed by other users, potentially compromising user data and security.

25. Y

Yotta: A metric prefix in the International System of Units denoting a factor of 10^24 (1,000,000,000,000,000,000,000,000). It is the largest officially recognized SI prefix and is primarily used in scientific contexts.

26. Z

Zoning: In network security, zoning refers to the practice of segmenting a network into different areas to improve security, manage traffic flow, and isolate sensitive data.

In the ever-evolving landscape of networking, the role of a network administrator is both challenging and rewarding. Mastery of the terminology outlined in this chapter is crucial for anyone aspiring to succeed in this field. By understanding these terms, network administrators can better communicate with colleagues, troubleshoot issues, and design robust network infrastructures. Continued learning and adaptation to new technologies will remain essential as the field of network administration progresses.

As technology continues to evolve, the glossary of terms and concepts intrinsic to network administration will similarly expand. This chapter should serve not just as a resource for current terms but as a stepping stone toward a more profound understanding of networking's future developments.

Index